Bonny Cassidy | Final Theory

New Poems

GIRAMONDO POETS

Bonny Cassidy | Final Theory

First published 2014
from the Writing & Society Research Centre
at the University of Western Sydney
by the Giramondo Publishing Company
PO Box 752 Artarmon NSW 1570 Australia
www.giramondopublishing.com

Designed by Harry Williamson
Typeset by Andrew Davies
in 10/16.5 pt Baskerville

Printed and bound by Ligare
Distributed in Australia by NewSouth Books

National Library of Australia
Cataloguing-in-Publication data:

Bonny Cassidy –
Final Theory / Bonny Cassidy
ISBN 978-1-922146-61-8

A821.4

To Tim Grey,

reader, husband and co-conspirator

Other books by Bonny Cassidy

Certain Fathoms

Acknowledgements

This book's research and composition was generously supported by a Marten Bequest Travelling Scholarship for Poetry. The final section of Part I was commissioned by the University of Western Sydney and the Sydney Consortium for the *Biodiversity and the Arts* project in September 2010.

Some sections appeared as earlier versions in *Young Poets: An Australian Anthology* (John Leonard Press, 2011), *So Long Bulletin* and *Jacket2*.

I thank the following for permission to reproduce material in this book: Margaret Edgcumbe; HarperCollins Publishers Australia Pty Ltd; Angela Rockel; Petra White; Brook Emery; Graeme Miles; John Mateer; Lionel Fogarty; Tony Thomas; Tim Wright; Sarah Day and Jill Jones.

All efforts have been made to obtain permission to quote from James K. Baxter, 'Pig Island Letters', *Collected Poems*, ed. Paul Millar, Oxford University Press, 2004.

I am grateful for John Leonard's early support and editorial advice on Part I. Thanks to Duncan Hose for reading a version of the manuscript; and to Catherine Cassidy and Vijay Khurana, my travelling companions through the Nullarbor and Tasmania, as it unfolded.

'Ranges and countless channels uninhabited
country decades, is not weird
cones
knives, volcanoes borning a surface external
wave, rock over arid plains are not far from our base.
The crashed mass perfectly dry aired, raised rim
made outer vanished whirling, high speed actually happens'

LIONEL G. FOGARTY, 'Scenic Wonders – We Nulla Fellas'

'Nothing happens, and it keeps not happening forever...
on the long road from order to disorder.'

BRIAN COX AND ANDREW COHEN, *How The Universe Will End*

*

A camera tracks the ocean floor
(eating images, not colliding). And rests.
Sial plumes in its wake, starfish
snake from ridge to trench.

A child plunges headlong into that valley
scuttling crud.

The camera is her dream tunnel.

White tentacles flare; the child hardly budges. She sleeps.
Her nails grow.

One letter at a time. I write her out.

I

Yesterday was, think, to one line descends.
Not quite.

At dawn, the mess of trees produced stars.
The radio gave thanks for another – found the week before,
    300 times our sun.
They said it could be heaved closer,
to understudy our panting source.

In classrooms children drew the procedure – colossal ropes and
    lake-sized mirrors.

And here it is: morning again, and again
forcing itself through the leaves
inhaling space.

Once, during a Roy Andersson film I saw celluloid burn that way.
First, the sound departed and the room went still; then
shimmering rocked the screen like heated oil; before a dark pupil
burst the scene and grew.

They'd kept it a surprise;
popping the moon
to clear the new sun's path,
discourage the trebling oceans.

After the last tide, our orbit
locked back into place, we clinked glasses.
The coast held together a while,
the detritus of the old harbours
unmoved upon floodlit Earth.

*

Underneath
ongoing day

the day goes on:
trucks roam for exploration play.
They rummage

layers staked on time's dart like a Valentine

splintering
the rifts
of scissored liquid.

Above it all:
me in your apartment, shimmying
rocksteady.

*

Sleepless piff –
we wake to cars shaving
the coast road.

Lumpen contractions grasp the cliffs,
the acid sea balloons.

Your earth waves, waves bristle into a straight red streak

like distant resolutions
returning
shear
to the surface,
magma sponge.

If there's land it bubbles. Its subtle lip, its slumping bowl.
Water furies the pores. Ah lahar.

Whatever might, has been.

*

I ask if you remember –
before our specks clumped in the sky's roaring gaps –
in that other age of loneliness
when we spread like rafts of seed

just flecks of pace
pinching together. Ink without words.
When we started to think, so much
that we cooled ourselves stiff.

And turned to tell our twins and twins of twins, but their faces
were only drafts bruised with life, cast in chill

and we turned, edges furred,
became a disc of beach hammered black and blue.

Can you think, away round that orbit,
to when we gutter and wisp, and spit?

'We'll drive 'til this land swims,'
you say. 'My camera might sink
but we'll be safe inside it:
fat and rich and pink.'

*

We take the mountain road
behind the dislodged crust –
your first time in my car.

The slopes are white and black, on black.

Movements worm across the tar
on their chests; eyes down
we drive over them, facing the peak.

The peak drags closer,
crackling my radio to dust.
Telegraph wires
swing into gradual forgetting

as I search the rear window
for a final perspective –

but end is only an idea, diffused
into a ranging sheet of light.

Instead I see her: my heartless twin; useless thing
pulsing behind the paper in my hands.

*

We close the drapes
of the Summit Motel.

Gold the spill
of felt. I hold it, glassed;
peer above the rim at you –
patiently watching my chin, where
a droplet cruises,
and gripping the carafe –

at you in the mirror behind
gripping the carafe.

Blood darkens, throat frills:
water folding under weed;
the landscape fading
to its frame; light
sets leaden at the window.
I breathe into the glass. You fill.

*

When we emerge from the empty motel
we are small again,
the ground makes itself known.
Keys drop onto an unattended tabletop.   We drive
into the loose gauze of frozen sun.
Our tyres smoke where no cars have gone.
Wire and cardboard work up through the heath.

Death now seems a detached curiosity. We talk
unmetaphorically, climbing the bends
between scrub and a string
of pickets lunging into the cloudhead.
As we turn and turn,
we don't speak about that pitch
but know that you, the passenger, can foresee
whatever I can only imagine.
In the 50s
the teens in this valley
were accused of promiscuity
led by bored girls who agreed to almost
anything.
Finally
we land, unable to see back;
and pull up in a vacant town to pace the kerb and breathe in long
straight lines.

*

Asleep at the wheel, I listened to the zone we'd left – scorched sea
rushing its gaps – and heard something

fall to the bottom of the universe.
The car door opened.

You'd raided the pharmacy, rattling more canisters of film.

Ocean eggs, puha, pork and kumara.
The Maori owned the land. I have a camera.

Tonight you make the darkest room.
The photos you retrieve are a scream –
heart-battering reams of fortune and shadow.
Your finger squinting the aperture
and the flint of your lens raised

have imposed a double: lichen and hub cap
printed across one another

like two hands braced against the light, a herald for the
Anthropocene.

Bucking
under
distant melt

talking to itself
this chain of push

an envelope of land
is opened and warm-skinned
cold-blooded ocean welling.

One word at a time, see the little bastard coming to the fray.
An inkling child of oil and grit

must lack solidity, be eroded
less than lithograph

beginning somewhere
not in me.

*

Last night we ate the *titi* and its feathered oil.

We wake in a crush, hook to wing, half-buried
in our own beach. Light gouges the Pacific.

Steering beside its flash, we're saturated
by plenty, and still want more. Are there others,
scattered – hungry like us, better dressed?

From far off we watch Earth's guts
slope up for air. In a knot they well beneath the ozone tear,
simple as silhouette.

Clouds and islands enter, exit.

Trailing for water, our footsteps are cased in ash;
it sets around oyster, foam
and a small pool of air, tripped open.
Only night can rip its stare from the sun.

A band shell flickers
by the shore of coloured globes and bones,
its humpback turned against the nearby broken bluff.
Footlights fail inside
its rose-painted throat: a ridged tunnel of heat.

Before us, behind us, and no one to speak.

*

The quiet day
comes; it glows with us
and no one.

Its west wind boughs
and flocks the street: once, it brought the rifleman, bush wren,
rock wren, Steven's Island wren, piopio, huia, saddleback, kokako,
short-tailed bat, long-tailed bat –
who opened a gap and thudded through, back-first.
The place became
a host of wings, a fall of parrots. Spur-wing plover, black-fronted
dotterel, white-faced heron made branches and needles ring. Coot,
grey teal, welcome swallow, wax eye.
Once, a single spoonbill lost in snow.

I gather kindling from last night's gale;
some for fire, but most is green and soft.
Now birds are pinned on roads, wind showers turning
over their wings.

For every hit there is a family of misses – the waste that breeds chance.
Perhaps, far from these gusts and double-glazed
in aircon, lie the hits:
their retired feet, claw to ceiling; beaks lightly gaping
under fields of plastic wrap, their boneless bodies saved.

Silverfish and beetle would prosper there –
unaware that, just as they are trundling memories of deeper time,
they eat memory into even, mealy clumps.
Their kind is also righteous here:
hot peals of insects are the sum of our swarms.

You build the fire
warmer than deserted rooms. You char feathers off the broken birds.

Marvell, Berger talk of being eaten with their lovers
into pure porridge & honest bone: is this what you desire, too –
your camera steadfast throughout, its reel
unwanted by worm and roach?

No – picture us
against a tree, its crown
the last blaze on a valley floor.
It's cold. And around the corner
is night, with its sliding walls.
Stringy conifers seam the light.
Dimming silently.

That is how it goes, I think: not femur to femur
but minute to minute; or gone already, while you focus
these tongues of flame and, impatient with chance,
arrange your film around evening.*

* If we lay
beneath that rubble
we'd see how we were built for ruin
like sand for glass.

For now, you are a still.

And in some future ocean our beloved proteins will
roll, perhaps finding one another, linked
by a theoretical wave
like voices sent through cans and string.

II

The first thing she recalls
is the sweep of wind and water,
an arm of plastic gametes
ushing about her. They circle
and she clings to their raft

face to face with a rubber alligator

then wheels, seeing
the alligator dissolve as she grows:

byproduct, polymer-spun
and grasping.

The sea responds with holes. If this is it,
if there is nothing more, then nothing more must be more,

what is not cannot be. Hold my hand.

*

The child passes from one sea to another
or moves half a mile.

The water
flowers, flushing
weed and jelly into view.
The child skims it with a carry-bag, and chews.

        Gently the ocean
simmers her legs.
There is, has always been

        a pang of disintegration
which she dips and pats with carbonic fizz.

When the sun arcs
she tents herself
in hair

as a cross-hatched passenger, holotype
staring through strands.

        Skin floats from her hands. Hollow sky.

The child gets by.

*

Squinting a long bright burr on the horizon

she senses beneath her
the clicking of light through water
        a crop of greens.
        Overturn, pluck, surface –

cliffs buckle into focus and wince. They stain
the water with grains
swelling beneath, barely matter

writhing in the shallows.

*

In a crevice beneath the cliffs
splashing shade
raising herself

the child lurches

for a hold on a lip.

As the crevice narrows, water thins
where it must: following

          she collapses
          the air inside her,
     particulates and flows
               outside the sun.

*

The child is an erratic.

Idling on the polished lip, pushing her hair
into its whorls.

Pretending to understand why the ocean ends
here. Drinking from the teeth
of the cliff.

Or lying crooked in the sun, eyes open,
unmoving as it grates
across her body.

She misses polystyrene in a storm –
the way it popped above the waterline
and shed itself. The taste and quiver.

The ocean's a mouthed thought.
The ocean sits in the corridor.

*

Around sockets and nostrils
through their straws of sun
        unmaking, made

The cliff props itself up, its piles of age and buried faces

        her legs fidget
                lime-dusted, kicking air

        she rests in a gapehole
and traces over faded red scrawl: SUCK   SHIT

*

White wind. The child climbs

her acres of hair clear as rain
down the cliff.

*

Behind her shivered legs, the cliff.
In front: gibber crumble, swinging forward through the heat

and white soil, into which
her complicated body
quakes

moths and flies.

The flies eat the moths –
crashing them slowly
mid-air –

and when they've clustered on a corpse she snatches
at the crowd, fills her mouth, cancelling their fuss
with her fried tongue.

But in the landscape of her head
one lives on, tapping –

she rolls outside-in
she flaps

nipping at space

between the rocks –

and props

at the mouth

of an opening, a sink
her own size across, sledged into the earth

licking down grains and stones.

She shoves her head into its void –

the buzzing of the colony
hangs back –

water pours out of her face
into the dark

and she sniffs –

leans in further, to hear –

a child's sniff –

I'm switching the poem off and on;
it's not a pet, after all, but a function.
Scapekid. Widget. And she knows how
to thicken like a pause, glaze over.

*

A moment, a year
since she felt the presence
of her skin.

Now it's always night already.

The cave crawls.
Stone claps its lines round her ears – and that dripping in her lungs, water blinking

patterns breeze
place
unravels moving

She draws
a wide circle.

*

She draws wide
away from where she fell.

When water blows thick and flat
into the cave, the ceiling runs
with hollow slaps
and calcium panic.

Then the rain will end,
and twists of heat.
The child will wrap hair
around her legs and feet;
lump it from nape to pad head
and pack herself up, neat.

She inches ahead

when a coin of sunlight sails
onto the dark before her

like new,
rippling as she approaches.

Marking it

she's led into a fuzzy pool

and the dish of light breaks, spreads
broadening until she slides
    into its ring, breath and hair
    scrambling up
    over one another
    toward the pinhole

    above.

    She feels its small grin on her cheek.

*

Crisp bugs plummet through its beam
and the child chucks herself at them, munching.

She watches waxy shawls
tapering down around the pool

as the pick of light casts
        through their solid gush

        hardly noticing that it smatters
and then swallows itself up – one day passing

back up into dark.

Gripping the pool's surface
she finds its dry edge.

        Her fumbling hand
                clasped
        in porous reply.

*

Clutching the clutching thing, she follows
its thumb, down the double bow and hinge
        of an arm.

        It lifts
from a scree of rubbish and shell.

The child flops
out of the pool, onto her front.
When squeezed, the hand's knuckles pop
into her palm.

She worries at them with her gums,
gazing into a blank screen.

III

We drive on for high ground, and on.

After a while of sleepy drift
the earth had turned violent
again, time's javelin sped.
One night, fed up with crickets
and fetid parrots we tore
and ate Marvell and Berger.

Our minds dream fabulous lies – of the real
we remember only shudders.
Think of a crowd and, between your eyes,
try to make its faces out: they're deserted,
a place you visited once but never photographed.

We drive to the high ground: south, our only point.

*

'I dreamt a cavalcade – some plodding feet, some trashed sedans –
trundling into twilight forest.
We were backseat; a neighbour or cousin
steering us under the dark.

In one of the cars some kids
amped their dying stereo
so it shone across the valley.

As a lake came into view
they played Buddy, and your glasses flashed like gibbous moons.
The lake was an ellipse; matte ink
shielded by a clip of sand.

A biplane lifted from its beach and wiped up light,
cue:

a dam wall,
exquisite curve.

The lake rose, floating
on the valley
then deepened to a stop.
Sailing peaks.

We flickered.
The new lake was real, we were fake.'

*

'Around this bend – '   We dust
a road along the margins of my dream;
our stupid map potholed by silverfish.

Empty jerrycans cough
from the trailer as I steer us
through churned ash and tinder
a blue forest of nerves.

Occasionally a track veers, pinkish.

We stop at one, blocked
by webs of rope slung from ground to bough to crown,
and a dangling banner
TOOT FOR OLD GROWTH
flanked by two shanties
made of tarp and branch, folding chairs, donation box.
You slip a bottle-cap in, thudding cardboard. We pass.

*

Here the valley, loading from my memory
into stubble forest. Inside it, the speechless lake

now evaporated vision. Peaks wade in its remains.

We print our feet onto the cream sand,
siphon its puddles into the jerrycans,
glugging throatfuls.

Either poetry or a fracture could restart
the river's current: uncomplicate
                that concrete dam
                    just as these words cup
                    the old lake – still faintly carved and sunk –
                        and undo its eclipse.

*

Swerving from the valley's head
pipes cascade silently
and divert
to a compound buried in slick white rock.

The road screws into it
through a busted cyclone gate
(BUZZ TO ENTER)
down, until the rock's own light dims

and from a raft of neon strips
a last glinting bulb
shows the compound's gut.

Three stilled turbines balance the space like stupas.

The car locks itself in their magnetic knot.
I turn the key, half-expect
the room to shatter dry and weightless –

instead, your voice, talking us
back to the surface

as power disappears beneath quartz and schist.

*

First we see
the starry flags tilted:

the birds that exist always elsewhere –
in name and abandoned hole, on the wing, after hours –
having traded off a final, pencil descent
for the return
to buried darkness
and rest.

You ask me their name;
I say one quickly, invented;
it sits on the wind,
no less alive than another, no more
than the birds at our feet.

First we see the first birds in years.
Our tyres blur into sand.

*

From here to that faint point

a plain of sand   where a swamp
    gave itself up to sun:

    mummified smears of jellyfish and faded balls, hard hats
        stretch away into the sift and crackle.

        A town's sketched into the lee of the point.
        You hesitate, squinting for a glimmer
        of motion or light; I imagine us gliding
        through a supermarket.

        At last I hear your feet slide
        into the wake of mine.

*

Lumped onto the plain:
grey skin – its tinge
of blue remembered ice –
and one flyblown ventricle, an eye-sized welt.
Wind-cleaned tail and skull.

We circle for a jaw, a socket,
some anchor to its face and direction
of breath. No teeth;
instead a pincer head
and the arabesque beak of landlessness.

We walk its trail – a splayed drag –
                                        in reverse.

*

The point is a staunch plug,
collared by remnants of its town.

Water's long gone from Woolworths' sand-strewn aisles;
cans, a shovel, last batteries hang from our hands.

It might be Sunday. At the end of the main street
a tarred stump grins, eyes bored, triangular nose
and teeth carved from the timber's pale underflesh.
HE'S HISTORY, the plaque tells us,
light sawing through a gash above his painted brows.

We pause to see my Toyota's windscreen
across the plain, catching sun.
It reminds you of music,
and you try to make a song appear

in the space between our heads:
bobbing on the sand, your arms all over
some forgotten beat.

*

Town doors locked, unlocked.
In a bungalow of cannibal roses
we stuff the landlord's library into a grate,
watching the novels whinge and fox
before they brighten the room.
                    'Degenerate.'

You're strung on the thought of a rare volt
or two. Sneering at the wall's dead faces,
you spill the new batteries.

I hide my books under the couch.
Day by day, the poem writes itself
but I give it form. Order and delay
cannot be made from space and time; how could they?
All my words are gunning for extinction, all they can tell us is:
        live more.

From this borrowed window
we scan the distance for the cyclone
that dumped those creatures in the sand.
Nightfall changes the place
from edge to sequence;
you can walk the edge of light
but I'm still watching how
the plain fills with carmine
while we wait.

*

I retch into the sink, woken and kicked.

There's a hum – a stir in the dormant power lines
or pipes, though the taps refuse to dribble.
The morning's shunted from town to plain;
you must be out already
hunting the streets.

In the kitchen I sit down by the jerries
dappling the walls with blistered patterns.
Admiring your pyramid of Skim Carnation tins
I drain a slow storm of white
sugar: filling the apex of your empties
then faster, the tiers.

Our front door swings open to the street's breeze
and I can see, down the passage

an advertisement above the milk bar
a Viking's head, tanning
– VALHALLA –

and behind him, that hum.
Hunching forward thinly, it runs.

*

I find you, sheltered from the wind
inside delicate, umber romanesque:
a church just briefly, now papered and shelved
with local hoards.

Bits have fallen off the maps.
Behind the door, bullroarers swing
above a pair of china boats. Strips
of gravy stick inside their lips.
I sign the guest book.

Along the back wall: a monument
of fridge magnets, screaming posters and front page splashes.
You frown at a photo of marching crowds stretched
the width of a city street.
'Remember that?'
I shake my head.
'Me either.'

*

Everything echoes,
the dead and those not yet born returning,
speech in fragments like a gust of bells.

The track climbs around the point.

Draped about us, the stink
of shells of burnt ash fat;
smell of last night, last
century –
        gaps in the ground
where signposts would have
told us

                    instead
we shuffle amongst boulders
the colour of old fires,
clean as knowledge.

Down there
behind buttongrass
and mineral, is that
the rising syntax
of smoke
dot-dash-stop?

Or midges, tying the air in knots.

Those fires were soft – we can tell
from this point and its carefully
folded rocks.

*

I forget my body for hours;
at times it's all I can think.
Part of me is heavy; resisting the trudge
I pull against it, toward you
carrying the maps and camera. 'I heard sighing last night.'

Nearing the point's flat top
you draw out map and pen
already craning for a river or a full lake
        while in the noon sun I see
only our limbs ahead, groping.

Then in the red loam, a web of burrows
gaping open and feathered by the wind.
And a sign here names the bird, as you wanted;
not as I named it, but rounded and agile,
the language still warm. We roll it
into our sentences, but it hardly makes a sound.
        I take it out of the poem and put it back on the ground.

Clods of soil fly
north, back across the plain
to the car's chrome winking by the dunes,
and the sun-stripped hills, the stubble valley,
whatever came before

back, across the grains and aeons curled in our cells

a family secret, past stone and sand which say
that the only way to go on forever
is to become as small as nothing at all.
Water milk wine fall into the ground
like smoke rises thinning.

Our south, rimmed by glare
bouncing between the cloudless sky
and slipping earth.

You haven't touched the maps.

*

Hunger and brandy eat sleep
and leave me standing
by the window, again; opaque.
We frame a scene of settlement, even
now.

I watch you deeply gone
into the bed behind me, and recall how today
you turned the camera in your hands,
supposing it was flotsam.

The poem and the photo are desire
collected, dispersed. As each boulder
found its lodgement here,
so it prepares to shift. So we look in
silently at ourselves.

For no good reason I wipe sand from the sill.

*

This morning we work indoors, shuffling together
pages and prints; dry eyes cast aside from the window

until you lead mine up to its frame

See how the characters emulsify
into the blue, now vacuous, nondescript.
Things fall apart.

and that placid, pointless view. Like it
my poem will tear and curdle, taken onwards

washed of use,
reversed.

*

A few possibilities could happen
next, but anyway

when the plain starts
to speak the poem
shrugs. She tears off on the tide.

*

Above the forgotten shore
rise car roof and trailer:
magic carpet.

*

The point packs down
rumples under the plain.
By now, the lake must be full again.

*

We go
into the sough

of stopless
beginning

the sea turns on

and your glance
levers open
the borrowed land

hold my hand

we rush in.

IV

Her dormant fingers tell
bulbs and spasms in the pool;
inside her long dream they appear
as sound and colour.

A burning spear moving horizontally between trees through
complete darkness.

She wakes. The ceiling feels closer to her head. Snaps ring
prising open the cave, pounding bundles

her eyes like asterisks
tick up at a blast laddering

the cave's mouth, half-drowned

and her face
to the immoveable

sky cut from stone, stone from sky.

The ocean's got her by the hair
and through sudden green
over daylight's electric line

*

The open water slows like a memory coming on

gushes from her
empty, full.

Empty: rubble leaking.

Held a moment by flailing kelp
she croaks –

the voice wings around a pillar
and back to slap her mouth

full: let go.

She tries breathing with the peaks.
Folding into wells, they wait for her, forget.
Hocking, she tracks her liquid as it joins the spume –
how far her eyes can pick it morphing white then blue –
and sees double, one lens pressing upon another.

Back there, her cave
open and hardening to a whistle.

*

A block of blue
passes before her, chained to the water,
groaning low, high.

Figures crawl over it: thoughts trailing behind,
their insistent arms heap up the plastics she has loved.

The west wind shoves.
Already distracted from the nearby animals

she lets herself be taken over

valleys.

*

A twisted stomach queals and
listing, she gulps enough brine

to sink

onto a rift shelf piled with trash.
One thin scrap bends gently from the heap

its still-tinted image (miniature sky, corner of lake)
too fine for her gravelly eyes.

She eats it. Guts racing, she drops like a breakbone

down the rift
(past a rusted box, its long eye gazing into sludge)

to the heavy water, where she lands.

Someone loved someone at some other time.

Dizzy, weighted to the floor
she picks at a spread of morsels not seen since her lives
on the surface: canisters, their reels of punctuated weed.

She reaches through the wall
of a small cavern
and takes a seat beside the wheel,
        dozy when the dark gets in.

*

Thought dissolves into strings of

black smokers hurl
the trench
up into a ridge –

transparent
limbs sawing away
at blindness – climbing

mounds of shells
huff curly gas
and settle in its fug.

She comes to –
thirst not her own, a tickle in her spine.
Rummaging the hadal scum
she rips white clams from their roots
and sifts with toothless gums.

TOYOTATOYOTATOYOTA she copies
in the silt, over and over the shapes crashing out.

*

She rises.
A grain of light shines
through the depths
as her blood rows steadily under its course.

Ascending,
this figment, our scrap
sheds particles;
drained into frazil, she shrinks.

Her bellows grind through avenues of the last ice,
breath-bags rush from her mouth
up cryptic distances

she follows

licks the light
and sticks.

Nose to sloppy ice
she gnaws –
a line draws itself

across her head
and silently folds
inward:

the thin zones inch

she rises
involuntary

*

In bergy soup
the ocean melts from chips and horns.
She recognises her raft of litter
growing, gathering its bower
from the tepid chop.

Shapes hang dimly beneath the floes –
weed whips, tiny cliffs and frozen rails of light
come forming out of seltzer.
Every floating fraction seems familiar –
plosion, gill
stem
quilt

buried in a ground below the mind.

Night's lost over an edge she loses:
sundogs slurp on the jellied water, angular glances

spin off tilted planes
and sputter
cones of nonsense.

She's looking into rooms, hollow wrecks
of sunken floors, rents and passages.

They scratch to a halt. Quietly falling.

As she rolls
in a runnel between them,

now and only once
she sees her face:

        numb and badly made
in the floe's submerged fringe, dipping

in the water behind her eyes
behind her feet, glowing

on and down.

*

She clambers upside
a tabletop surfing on the water.

Slipping, her bones yaw in their case of skin –

she scrabbles the formica, hovers
before it tips

her onto a gabbro beach

flip.

*

Shadows reverse at speed
into cloud.

Down below, she lolls
on the mush. No flies, no
motion in her peripheral.
              (Standing, you'd see
              the stones tapped with scenes, superposed:
                   eyes and toes, ovals whirling inwards.)

Dragging her damp hair
she goes up the gulch
scraping over
dried remnants of strays –
worn leather, rare whiskers –
and coagulated moss.

She reaches a ridge above the beach;
and gawping back, fishing moss from her teeth,
unpicks the sequence:

a defrosted gulf
bouncing steely
dirt peeled to luscious pink

its groves of silver
breath and shredded flame

feed a gleaming pipe
a frieze of tiny lights
across black mud
sea
to a crowd of nudging carriers.

Knots of figures speak head to head,
passing words under the circling gale

filing out to the water over the water
past the pipe's lights
their long unblinking track
blundering from star to star

to where her narrow eye
reaches for Earth's sill –
marked by an arrow erected in the channel,
luminous then dim, like breath. Day is old.

Here, I thought, she
might speak – a language
of one – and so disappear
into meaning. No.
I wasn't here.

Back down through the wriggling moss, past
speaking stone and disused parts
arse-first into slush
    and under.

        The pipe's drawing out its fill,
        a casual twist of motion there
        all taken and all left by the carriers.

    Still the flashing arrow marks the deep

reflected weakly by the face
and shoulders now bobbing unseen
above the waterline.

Its cool accident. The face the gulf thinning
                                        out into a disc, unsaid

Notes

p.ix Lionel G Fogarty, 'Scenic Wonders – We Nulla Fellas', *New and Selected Poems: Munaldjali, Mutuerjaraera*, Hyland House, 1995; Brian Cox and Andrew Cohen, *How The Universe Will End*, Collins, 2011, and reprinted with permission of HarperCollins Publishers Pty Ltd.

I

p.5 Quotes Kendrick Smithyman, 'Felled Macrocarpas', *Selected Poems,* ed. Peter Simpson, Auckland University Press, 1989.

p.13 Quotes James K Baxter, 'Pig Island Letters', *Pig Island Letters*, Oxford University Press, 1966.

p.15 Paraphrases John Caselberg's poem, 'Van Gogh', *The Sound of the Morning*, Pegasus Press, 1954. Caselberg's lines, famously represented by the New Zealand painter Colin McCahon, read: 'God, it is all dark. / The heartbeat but there is no answering hark / Of a hearer and no one to speak.' *Titi* is the *te reo Maori* word for the muttonbird or short-tailed shearwater.

II

p.21 Quotes Brook Emery, 'After the lassitudes of blue', *Collusion*, John Leonard Press, 2012.

p.26 Quotes Petra White, 'Bunda Cliffs', *The Incoming Tide*, John Leonard Press, 2007.

p.31 Quotes Jill Jones, 'Dark Clangs Down', *The Beautiful Anxiety*, Puncher & Wattmann, 2013.

III

p.41 Quotes John Mateer, 'Visitors Centre', *The West: Australian poems 1989–2009*, Fremantle Press, 2010.

p.51 Quotes Angela Rockel, 'Remember: A working definition of blessing', *Salt* vol.16 (2002).

p.54 Quotes Graeme Miles, 'Libations', *Recurrence*, John Leonard Press, 2012.

p.56 Quotes Sarah Day, 'Sky Writing', *The Ship*, Brandl & Schlesinger, 2004.

IV

p.63 Quotes Tim Wright, 'Redactions II', *Redactions I–XII*, Chain of Pounds Press, 2012 <http://swimswam.files.wordpress.com/2012/03/redactions-i-xii2.pdf>

p.67 Quotes Hal Porter, 'Dry Final Scene', *Elijah's Ravens*, Angus & Robertson, 1968.

p.76 Quotes Wiliguru Pambardu, 'The First Truck at Tambrey', trans. Anthony Paul Thomas, *Taruru: Aboriginal Song Poetry from the Pilbara*, ed. Carl von Brandenstein, Rigby, 1975.

This project has been assisted by the Victorian Government through the Arts Victoria Developing Writers' Program and by the Commonwealth Government through the Australia Council, its arts funding and advisory body.

ARTS
VICTORIA